The Baby That Ate Cincinnati

The Baby That Ate Cincinnati

poems by
Matt Mason

STEPHEN F. AUSTIN STATE UNIVERSITY
NACOGDOCHES ★ TEXAS

STEPHEN F. AUSTIN STATE UNIVERSITY PRESS
PO Box 13007, SFA Station
Nacogdoches, TX 75962
sfapress@sfasu.edu
936-468-1078

For information about special discounts for bulk purchases, please
contact Texas A&M University Press Consortium sharon-mills@tamu.
edu or 800.826.8911

Cover Art and Design: Robb Blum

Manufactured in the United States of America

LIBRARY OF CONGRESS IN PUBLICATION DATA
Mason, Matt
The Baby that Ate Cincinatti / Matt Mason. — 1st ed.
p. cm.
ISBN: 978-1-936205-94-3
I. Title

ACKNOWLEDGEMENTS

Thanks to the following periodicals and anthologies in whose pages these poems previously appeared:

Bird's Eye reView-"Intro to Communication"

Black Star Press *2011 Nebraska Poets Calendar*-"Notes For My Daughter Against Chasing Storms"

burntdistrict-"What I've Learned, Being a Father"

Far From Home-"Note to a Friend: The Long, Dark Night of Your Dating Life," "Night Terrors," and "The Story of Ferdinand the Bull"

Grawlix Poetry-"We Break Bread With the Future"

Idiolexicon-"Ode to My Wife's Panties"

Laurel Review-"Decades Later, He Recalls the Terrors of Birth"

New Zoo Poetry Review-"Newborn"

Paddlefish-"The Baby That Ate Cincinnati," "The Theology of Parenting," and "When The Baby Falls Asleep, We Celebrate"

Sugarhouse Review-"September 21: Poem for Omaha," "A Brief History of Transcendence," and "Over You Like Water"

The Smoking Poet-"The Loveless Thesaurus"

Aim For The Head: An Anthology of Zombie Poetry (Write Bloody Publishing, 2011)-"13 Ways of Looking at a Baby (And please note: this poem has nothing to do with zombie movies)"

Chorus: A Literary Mixtape (MTV Books, 2012)- "Connections"

Filling The Empty Room (Morpo Press, 2010)-"The Baby is Very Busy This Morning"

High Desert Voices (The Wordsmith Press, 2006)–
"The Baby That Ate Cincinnati"

Mamas and Papas (City Works Press, 2010)–"Night
Terrors"

Pushcart Prize XXXVII: Best of the Small Presses
(Pushcart Press, 2012)–"Notes for my Daughter
Against Chasing Storms"

Slamma Lamma Ding Dong (iUniverse, 2005)–"The
Baby That Ate Cincinnati"

Contents

Chapter 3

TO SARAH, SOPHIA, AND LUCIA

CHAPTER 1

THE BABY THAT ATE CINCINNATI

Way they say it,
they say
                    baby
like a storm on the way,
they say   *baby*
like that's the cue for the thunderclap
to interrupt the wolves' long howls,
they say   *I got three*
                    and they're the best
            ever to happen to me
as they say
                    baby
same as you'd say "run,"
they shout
                    baby
like there are flames lickin' at the window frames,

            tell us
          how their lives
        didn't just change,
            oh no,

as
they
say
                    baby
like a hyena inside there
comin' out fangs a-blazin',
they say
                    baby
like it's standing
right
behind us,

that tornado on the highway,
                    but ain't
            it
        a marvel,

way they talk,
give that patronizing nod
when we
claim we still goin' to poetry readings,
we still goin' to see movies,
we still goin'
to call our friends
as they say
                    baby
like a bomb in the air,
they say
                    baby
like just waitin' in the shelter now
with AM radio and a can of pork n' beans

                    you're so lucky,
they then weep,
sincerely,

as I sit on the bed,
knees held precious,
watchin' my wife's belly,
bigger every day,
wonderin'
what's in there?

We gonna need a priest, a gun,
silver bullets, wire cutters, 16 gallons a hydrochloric acid,
Red Cross, National Guard, seven million dollars
in non-sequential unmarked bills

because all these warnings giftwrapped with blessings
when   I   know

ain't gonna be the same around here;
but

baby,

when we say "baby,"
let's say it
like we say "bread,"
like "honey,"
like "beautiful,"
like "dear,"
like it's true.

WAITING

We've been stubbing toes on cobwebs,
cutting our palms with spoons,
planning each corner like it's Everest's backside,
bruising our hands as we pick Q-tips up,
and then,
and then.

Because we've been stubbing our toes on cobwebs,
slicing our palms with spoons,
twiddling our thumbs until they snap,
holding books so tight that our fingers crack.

We are breaking our heads on pillows,
losing our voices reading the news,
her taut belly in the sky like a moon
as we sit on the porch
and stare up;

catching each other's hands
when, with wishes soft
on our tongues,
we fall
like stars.

CHAPTER 2

LEARNING TO BREASTFEED, 3:24AM

Oh, little demon scream,
we understand now
what soil grew stories
about changelings–good babies
stolen by spirits
and replaced with pumpkins
who howled like dogs
and drew blood
where they were offered milk;

the cowbird grown
in a nest of sparrows,
tiny bird exhausting
to keep this huge mouth
from bringing visits
by prim-eyeglassed social workers
so expert they can identify brands of baby powder
by the sounds of the granules
floating on air.

Oh, voice of madness,
of exorcism, of precious sanity
shaken for from empty pouches of sleep;
oh, eternal night
where even the butterflies
of rustle and soft gasp
ring iron bell-claps,
where every bed
sprouts the mad ascetic's sheet of nails;

we lie down stiffly,
counting
the clock's tick, tick, two,

tick,
tick,
tick,
three,
tick,
tick,
tick,
tick,

NEWBORN

Watch how newborns look around
at everything.
A yellow wall, a window frame,
a coat rack, oh sweet Jesus, a coat rack!

staring
like we would
walking through neighborhoods made of diamonds, tulips,
      or chocolate,
eyes turning full moon at every delicious

lamp post! weather-resistant vinyl siding!
They watch us, too, like something
fragrant, something invaluable, something
never-before; oh,

that water stain on the ceiling,
there's no difference between it and Cortez's Cities of
      Gold–
and,
you know,

I'm starting to see how this is true.
With newborn daughter in my arms,
I pace these same tired steps and
floors and

rooms and
watch her eyes go nova: who knew
some Michelangelo did my walls,
that Medicis secretly replaced my concrete floor with a
      luxurious reproduction!

Understand,
I do sneer at movies whose children over-
emote to make me weep, I cuss in traffic, grumble in lines,
turn my nose up at those who plan on voting for that moron
        in November; this

is not how I envision myself,
going all gumdrops and roses over cinderblocks and garden
        hoses;
but
I look at this wife and daughter some moments,

and I see rainbows
as if I've never seen such visions before,
like I
am so blest to be here on this futon of the gods.

And though we have all been raised to guard our stares:
tonight, I do look at you
and you
and you

as if there were no more meaningful sight: you
thought Twilight was high art, you
cut me off in traffic, you
will certainly vote differently than I, you

all glow like the saints in paintings;
and though there are too many days
when roads are nothing more than hard and grey, today
I look around me, today is,

today is more beautiful, wonderful, gorgeous, delectable,
        marvelous, miraculous
than any of the paper words I try to dress these fireworks
        in,

where pillow tags and ceiling fans are
revealed as the miracles they are,

like rose-soaked clouds brightening
at the small, brown board of horizon
where the skies
begin.

September 21: Poem For Omaha

There's just enough mist
for the lamp posts to masquerade
as tent poles tonight;

instead of spilling
down, they hold up
canvases of light.

And 30th Street shines
like a river under the moon
washing past brown thrift stores gone to bed,

because this city smells
beautiful, this city
of wet leaves

sticking like frescos
along the sidewalks, a masterpiece
the length of my city

that I remember–with a start
as I drive home, window down–
I love.

When the Baby Falls Asleep, We Celebrate

silently. My wife
comes into the light, arms high
and I jump up–
making sure not to creak the chair–
and we exult, we take off our shoes and we dance;
we are good people
shipwrecked on the shores of this strange island,
fearing the drums far, far through the trees;
we tiptoe across the beach, TV quiet
as if all the world must whisper,
must dare not wake her,
must bow to this new pharaoh
whose yokes we wear across our throats,
this thunder infant
with wrath grown as evening stretches
into the fury and the fussiness that nursing at the breast
can only sometimes abate;
and if she then wakes,
if the door creaks just so loud,
if it's you who made the toilet seat crack like a gunshot
        only moments after she went down and the woman
        who swore before Jesus to love you forever looks at
        you with all the flames of Hell in her eyes,
may God have mercy on you.

My wife and I rent nothing but horror movies now,
huddle next to the television trying our best
not to guffaw out loud
as these actors
face aliens, and disembowelments, things
we may have feared in another life;
but let's see Freddy or Jason or King Freaking Kong

make you fear
like when you only mean
to ease the door open thinking how beautiful
her little closed-eyes dream-face is
and instead see her sit up–
try not to scream–
her eyes rotate
to snap on your mortal form, oh, hah,
Godzilla, take a number, giant bug:
this monster is so monstrous
we don't even try
to run.

OVER YOU LIKE WATER

You never understand at the time,
that when she leaves you, when he leaves you,
your heart breaks
into song.

No, it never feels like it, as if your cheeks
will never dress in red again, but this
is your heart breaking
into blossom

as the seasons turn round,
as you realize you mistook February for May,
west for east as the sky skimmed past pastels
where your heart was breaking
into flight,

as you sat in a squeaking office chair, dripping formula
into rhyme, planting poems in undersized pots
until the night it all fell like rain
and your heart broke
into dance, broke free, broke open, yeah,

broke open,
broke bread with this future you look down from like a
        mountain
across those breaks so far below,
the ones that broke you
in

as you broke
out into this wife,
this baby breaking
like water across your shore.

Reflections on my 36th Halloween

Thing is, pumpkins speak so
softly, used to stand bright as billboards
with pyramid features and jowls shining,
and the seeds toasted to a luxurious crunch,

not gristly like these, not orange lip
curled inward, chapped black
with blue cotton sprouting
like cancers behind its eyes.

We all know
we are getting older,
but no one mentions
how even delights age

like bodies, their crispness
wearing from sprint to limp;
but,
still,

we light the candle,
drip the wax, and,
with a warm hand,
place it in.

step back.

WHAT I'VE LEARNED, BEING A FATHER

is that being a person
takes practice.
Nobody springs fully-formed anymore
like in ancient stories. Even Jesus,

we acknowledge, drudged through
the relative embarrassments of infancy:
arms as novel and unwieldy as tentacles,
no sense of social control with your tongue,

these brand new bowels
and the surprises they prove capable of;
these bodies
like rowboats on stormy seas,

crashing against momentum and seeming never,
ever will they be something
you can steer.
You may someday know

how to balance on water; but
for now
the waves do not answer
to your spastic, sausage-like hands.

WE BREAK BREAD WITH THE FUTURE

We, born without internet, cable TV, cell phones, CDs,
whose planets learned to make microwave popcorn
and eat meals in their cars,

we who have scrabbled up from prehistoric childhoods,
grown up to have nieces, nephews, sons and daughters,
          now,
their tiny necks barely able to bob those large heads up

for now;
we wonder, soon, how soon,
will they soar through the atmosphere like sparrows,

laugh at our quaint recollections
of archaic boundaries
like gravity, like matter, like mortality.

THE BABY HATES SUNSET

She throws the dark air
of her lungs out into the dusk, her
face red as the clouds. The baby
hates sunset, she
is weary
of laughing all morning, all
afternoon, she squeezes her face
into a fist, mouth wide to
blow at this last mist of sun.
The baby hates sunset and
she has no problem, yet,
speaking her mind, she
is in touch with her feelings, her needs, which,
in its way, is admirable;
    though I'd like to go to the Christmas party.
But the baby hates sunset, hates twilight,
hates carseats, hates hats,
hates singing, hates swinging, hates you, hates me,
hates being held
this way
and this way
and this way and this way and
this August-born greets the abbreviation of days
shrinking toward her first solstice
with hot licks of flame.

THE THING ABOUT NEWBORNS IS

The other mystery
of Easter Island, the one

that is not the square-faced monoliths,
is their written language.

An archaeologist named it
Rongo Rongo. Every newborn

I've ever met
is written

in this.

Night Terrors

She's started screaming at night,
this baby, gums shredding
with teeth, diaper filled up;
even so, that's old news, this
is bad-Bible-chapter terrified,
slasher-movie-girl terrified,
end-of-the-world kind of alarm, then
as her mom and I run
out of buckets out of rope out
of the thin bone of composure,
she drops back to sleep
like a snowflake sliding to a stop,
our eyes wide, flashlights popping
at every creak in every corner.

A Brief History of Transcendence

When the colored lights come out,
they fall as many as snowflakes
on downtowns and neighborhoods,
all somehow for that Jesus guy;
    because the stories about salvation,
    they're the best ones.

That baby in the manger is so everywhere,
dozens on all the store shelves, lit
on windowsills, lawns, and rooftops,
every December
    you look up
    and see him, look

and see so much of him
he seems common as the moon,
so familiar you lose him
in all that bright landscape.
    Hold on to hope and wonder, hold
    on to miracles and mercy,

our lives all have it, if we look, a moment
after millennia of legends, myths, debate, and
      experimentation,
that moment bursting through
once in the history of yourkind,
    that rocket journey, that remarkable step so ponderously
      planned out and
    still unexpected

when it arrives: atmosphere falling
like rain, hours and hours trembling
through engine after engine's drop,
your breath realized as a miracle
    landing you on the surface of a spotlight,
    amazed

at the scope, the expanse coalesced too briefly in the bare
        bulb
floating in your kitchen, splashing these ordinary cabinets
with something suddenly more, you rocking
in the uneven chair, palms flat on the bare table, you
    staring back at the earth
    so incredible there above you.

Decades Later, He Recalls the Terrors of Birth

It is so overwhelming,
this ice discovery
of a million colors more than black and red,

this tan slab that cracks
your newly-found rump to pink, sudden
smells and tastes whose bushels and hectares don't have
        words

yet; the world
used to be shaped
like you

and now, too much;
and for all this space, Jesus,
whatfor? the noise, sound, clatter

has lost the beat like it never had it,
running in front of, behind, across from the rhythm
and never

again in step.
It's no wonder
when your everything finds out the sun

doesn't really orbit the earth,
the sky
doesn't even orbit the sun,

and you,
you,
you,

it's no wonder
you won't speak right
for years.

INTRO TO COMMUNICATION

She can't use words yet.
She can smile, she can clap, she can say "Beh,"
delights in seeing you
return a smile, a clap, a "beh beh beh,"
electrified by the novelty
of communication. Imagine
yourself talking like this. You
could be in a Mongolian airport,
a Namibian lamp store
or the planet's loudest disco,
you just want to chat with

anyone and this is all you have.
For her, this is
the world. She claps.
I clap.
She smiles.
I smile wide.

Yesterday, she recited a poem to me,
it went:
        clap
        clap clap
          "beh beh
      beh"   clap
        "beh"
              clap clap
                clap
      smile.

Yeah, I know. It is
sad

for me, published poet,
creative writing teacher,
to see my eight month old so starkly
outdo me,
like I am the campfire and she
is the sun; I, the racehorse and she,
light; I,
scribbling simile
after simile what she
can give you
like that.

BEDTIME STORY

I used to live across
from the elevators, used to
live near the train tracks

but sleep
still came to my bed
every night,

left her black dress on the chair,
left her bright jewels on the nightstand
and washed against my skin until we were out.

Now,
I sit in bed
and watch her;

she holds the baby,
paces and rocks, she
drinks coffee and cries

into her toast some mornings,
she rocks and paces and
whenever she stops,

the baby howls
and howls
and howls.

THE LOVELESS THESAURUS

Roget is pissy tonight,
his book moves from loutish to lovelorn,
skipping over the words we need.
No "loveable," no "lovely,"
certainly no "lovemaking."
Maybe he's hoarding words,
plucking the more valuable
to stack in a vault, leaving us
to flip pages, after midnight,
by ourselves on those sofa-things,
the ones that seat two—it seems
there's a word for it, but—
not finding what we need, we mumble
"boorish, oafish, cloddish, dense,
churlish, clumsy, stupid, rough," on
to "bereft, rejected, jilted, forsaken,"
the ashes in our fireplaces grey
as ash.

Love Is

two people, both slightly more
striking than you, oblivious
to the camera

and the storefront
and the river
of passers-by.

Sometimes it does look like
those two naked cartoon characters
in my hometown newspaper

each morning, thrilled by the wonder
and wackiness in their sex-
organ-free lessons

until the days you spend curled
around a metaphorical toilet
sweating to retch out the heart
that is drumming against your guts.

You see, it is vague
enough to be both
alpha and omega, many
splendid thing and dog from hell;

for Heaven's sake, it
could be a poem, a god,
a pet cat, a supermodel,
Willa Cather, a barely-chilled can of Diet Coke on not even
        that warm a day
so

maybe you need to clarify your lexicography,
maybe it's misspeaking

to reference it
in terms of the efficacy
of a barely palpable
brush of her toes

as they stroke your shins under the sheets,
baby breathing steady in her crib
after a back-breaking day;
maybe the word is
wrong, garbled, misleading,
maybe you're too tired
to think of another word to say

as your hand sails across her stomach
and you pull her along you
just
to breath
her hair
as you drift
away.

So Sophia

So
Sophia makes music,
Sophia says ga la la,
Sophia says sounds
like meteors, bright
across the living room's sky.

Sophia lifts
her voice
like peaches,
Sophia sings
like birds do–no,

her song's the bird;
Sophia, she pins wings
on her whispers
and watches, laughing,
how they fly.

LISTENING

Cloudbursts crackle
across the cartop and windshield,
baby daughter in her seat
breaths her sleep deeply,

car parked, no rush
to disrupt any of this
by rattling doors, unbuckling her
from her snores, splashing in
to another store. There's time
to sit
and listen
to the singing

of rain
and dreaming.

ODE TO MY WIFE'S PANTIES

Roses on silk, red eye patch,
you mask too tiny to disguise:
I am on the bed, Neruda's "Every Day
You Play" on the open page between my legs,
this is the poem closing:
            "I want
                to do with you what spring does with
                            the cherry trees."
    And my wife walks through.
Wearing only you
and the baby nursing on her chest.
    Remember, Panties, remember pregnancy?
remember last year
where biology itself was birth control
and I would pull your smooth strings
down her soft skin,
across the kiss of ankle bones
to drop you by the bed,
the couch,
the sink, the car,
the cash register, the beautifully-trimmed lawn at the State
            Capital,
your touch sweet foreplay,
you bright flag flown
for me
to find comfort in;
    and before that,
remember honeymoon, remember
the drama of arguments
about something we've forgotten,
    but I still remember
after, seeing you

like a wink,
like a secret signal
that all is clear,
that this is time
to make up
and to kiss;
    oh, Panties,
I just want to be forgiven,
to forgive that way;
    but she comes to bed
and there are no raised voices,
no slammed doors,
all regrets left
in some other house;
we, new parents,
we just haven't slept
enough, not last night
or the night before
or last week
or last month
or, or, or;
  I reach quietly
to touch you,
fall asleep,
my palm
against your cheek.

Rememberizationing

You haven't been out like this
since the baby was born: alone,
night highway, middle of
Nebraska, moon so bright you could turn
off the headlights, one star–
maybe a streetlight–obscure
radio station playing something
with Middle Easterny cello;

the place you were
supposed to stop is miles
behind, you watched
the lights slide away
as you shot through,
hot day gone, you,
hand in the wind,
could drive till morning

and when that sun comes looking,
when that sun pulls up
over Kansas or Oklahoma, who
do you think'll be the most
surprised?

The Theology of Parenting

At some point
you can't take it:
when the baby won't go to sleep,
rolls around tired
like a drunk who doesn't know
they should just go home to bed,
whimpering, bawling, throwing her head
at everything in the room.

So everyone tells you:
let her cry
herself to sleep.

It makes sense
because you're slipping
because it feels like you're going
to find your bags packed
and a ticket to Crazy folded in your pocket
as that baby drops her head
against the floor and howls,
smacks her head on a chair leg
and howls, cracks her head on your head
and howls.

Here's what everyone says:
Put her in a crib.
She will cry.
Be strong.
Poke your head in every five minutes.
Be strong. Don't pick her up.
Just assure her
you're still there,
you're still rooting for her,

and one, two nights later,
she'll know
how to go to sleep.

And it makes sense,
as you pace, baby
squirming out of your hold,
you need to be up for work
in five hours and fourteen minutes,
you've got composure piled in your hands
like a dozen loose eggs, when one goes
it all tumbles
in splashes of mess,
so
it
makes
sense.

But you can't do it.

Can't sit watching Kimmel as if nobody's screaming,
can't let her cry
like a kitten outside your window
being tortured by pirates,

you barricade your sanity,
pray and build the walls up high,
whimpering like a,
well,
like a parent
at 11:58 p.m.

watching news on TV,
image and image and image
of full-color tragedy and folly,

of foreigners weeping,
of neighbors hugging their thighs and shaking,

of everything falling apart
like storm clouds into rain,
all of us,
all of us pounding the bars
of this crib, all of us left
to cry ourselves
to sleep.

Hold

Fathers hold their children, hold their tempers,
hold grudges, hold onto schedules
though the schedules shredded
by the time the sun burnt down.

Fathers pace in a.m. hours, carpet soft against callouses;
night lights, counter lights soft on atmosphere,
and the babies these fathers pace with,
they shriek, they twist, they blink, they

do everything
except the one thing this stiff dark asks.
Fathers are not monsters
if they growl. Fathers

are not monsters
if they kick the chair, throw
the pacifier, damn it: 3:28 a.m., alarm set to bang too soon,
same thing last night, same thing the night before, this

is for all the fathers, this
is for all of the roaring, the finger-tightening,
face-contorting, tongue-biting ones
who feel the full moon hot on their souls

and are
never
mistaken
for wolves.

THE BABY IS VERY BUSY THIS MORNING

The baby is very busy this morning, she
hurries about the house picking up socks and books and
          microscopic dots and
rushes back to hand them to you,

all the while, her face serious
as if she were deciding which wire on the detonator
to cut so that the dam doesn't blow.

You are not entirely awake; she
is motoring as if a coffee shop rodeos
inside her still-hardening skull, she

clearly has things to do, important things,
her "to do" list as long
as her arm,

well,
more so; reading:
chase the dog and jingle her tags;

check. Spill a small bowl of dry Cheerios across the floor;
check. Turn on the desk lamp with its cool circular switch;
check. Do it again;

check. And again;
check. Perfect this for several minutes;
check, check, check. Stop,

fart,
beam widely at this amazing accomplishment;
check. Unlock the secret of lever-style doorknobs;

not quite,
but it is only a matter of time as
she is so close;

and on and on, her nubby feet going
pat pat pat pat
across the kitchen floor,

circling you in your chair,
the black of every windowpane softening
to their inevitable, breaking light.

13 Ways of Looking at a Baby

(And please note: this poem has nothing to do with zombie movies)

I
On the night
when it commences,
you have no way of weighing
how much
your life
will be altered.

II
When you come upon her
as she finishes devouring;
her dinner sprayed across her face,
down her arms, in the tangles
of her hair; she will stare.
Open her mouth.
Gasp out:
"Gaaaaaaaaaaaa!"

III
She seems so slow down there.
You let your mind wander
just a squinch,
look back and, oh god:
danger!

IV
You only think she is down.
You feel like you've endured

a bone-jarring labor of Hercules but,
finally,
her eyes are closed,
finally
still.

Don't turn your back, watch her, the moment you turn away
    that cry will make your hair rise again, you will have
    to scramble back, find a way to put her down
again,
never be sure
when it all
may be finally
done.

                    V
It
is absolutely amazing
what she
will put
in her mouth.

                    VI
She smiles
and the teeth
in her head
look what's left
of a picket fence between the weeds
and the old dirt road.

                    VII
The dog

is always
the first
to get it.

VIII
They always give you some scientific explanation
how this all came about.
Yet, still,
you have to keep asking:
How did this happen?
What has brought this
here?

IX
The way she will look at you
sometimes,
as if she does not know whether you are air
or flesh,
her eyes wide and wild,
sparkle of saliva quivering on her chin
as she lurches
for you.

X
For as long as
you might live,
they
are yours
and you
belong
to them.

XI

She is so
very small,
it can startle you
how strong she really is.

XII

You will imagine her face, sometimes,
as if it can tell you the truth
about whether God exists or not, about what
sort of universe
we inhabit.

XIII

Ask the father or mother
stumbling through the house in the darkest of the night,
pants God-knows where:
they will tell you she has come
to eat
your
brains.

Connections

The highway passes through town after town after dark,
populations under each name announcing numbers
like 146, 217, 91, a mush of snow disappearing
against black pavement, you switch your high beams every few
      minutes
to be polite to the headlights floating your way.
You're close enough to start watching for motels, you go
to a high school tomorrow morning, 8:05, to talk poetry
though you haven't been able to put a good metaphor
in motion in months. AM radio fizzes,
you catch some Oklahoma City, some Chicago station
for a few lines before it shifts into buzz. FM rolls
on its own, the numbers keep moving, no place to stop.
The trains all move east tonight, high beams blaring, poetry,
you will tell them, connects worlds,
shows how one thing is so much like another
that we should be ashamed we ever missed it. You listen
to the tires squish and crunch and hum;
looking–headlights dingy with grime, slush smearing
across the windshield–
for metaphors.

THE STORY OF FERDINAND THE BULL

Dad would come home after too long at work
and I'd sit on his lap to hear
the story of Ferdinand the Bull; every night,
me handing him the red book until I knew
every word, couldn't read,
just recite along with drawings
of a gentle bull, frustrated matadors,
the all-important bee, and flowers–
flowers in meadows and flowers
thrown by the Spanish ladies.
Its lesson, really,
about not being what you're born into
but what you're born to be,
even if that means
not caring about the capes they wave in your face
or the spears they cut into your shoulders.
And Dad, wonderful Dad, came home
after too long at work
and read to me
the same story every night
until I knew every word, couldn't read,

                                        just recite.

QUESTION

When she asked that question, I was happy to feel
how much it didn't weigh, wasn't
a "Which came first," wasn't a "How much wood,"
there was no train leaving Omaha
at one hundred kilometers per hour.
That was everything else: her
near tears in a swivel chair, me
leaning against a cinderblock wall, baby
so thrilled with perpendicularity
that she runs and spins and will not lie down

until the movies we want to see leave theaters,
the playhouse we went to on that blush of an early date
        closes down,
till all our friends grow old, dress in plaid, and move to
        distant towns,
we, taping our TV shows and never watching them; no,

the question, the answer, really,
had heft like a snowflake on the glove
where it doesn't melt away;
hard to believe
by the look on her face
that I would be thinking about Chicago,
snapping a photo of her on the bridge, reckless,
        windblown smile
still on my–now our–refrigerator;
how we played hopscotch with state lines
in a way we now don't, stayed up late as wolves
without negotiations of who would change the morning
        diaper,

rubbed ourselves along one another in the ways
which cause such changes in our choices;

when she asked, when she said "Divorce" like it
was a book I might have read, well,
I said "No,"
same as you hold your tongue out for raindrops,
same as you watch for fireflies from the porch,
same as you pull your car off the paper highway
when, above the pine trees' silhouettes,
you see the colors Emerald and Red slow dance
in a way which fills you
with anything but doubt.

After We Saw That Penguin Movie, I Gave Thanks

for not being born a swimmer in Antarctica,
stumbling sixty,
seventy, ninety miles as winter hurtles down–
sixty, seventy, ninety below–to have sex

once a year;
hundreds of us hanging out like a Sun Myung Moon mob
          wedding on a glacier,
new wife soulfully staring into my small eyes
as she foots our new baby over, saying:

balance her on your feet, dear,
or she'll die. I'm going to go get some lunch. See you
in a month or two.
Try not to freeze to death

or you're a failure,
before she waddles to an ocean
far over the ice cap
somewhere, leaving me

to sway in the wind, surrounded
by shivering daddies,
no television, no beer,
just each other

and weather. Instead,
I sit at a kitchen table,
thermostat at sixty-seven, baby
bouncing on my knee, learning the word for "Whee!"

Penguins look less crazed, more
like little superheroes. I would carry this child
on bare feet if I had to, I would
keep the wind from touching her, fast

through blizzards, never give up,
never stop
till the iceberg
grinds through
that is stronger
than my heart.

At the Grocery Store, Valentine's Day

Men in heavy coats, brown, gather
around flowers
like we are tree trunks and this
a seasonless meadow in bloom
next to fresh tomatoes, grapes, and mangoes.

The men stand small and wide,
bundled tight against the February outside,
gaze through the roses,
the spring bouquets, the red,
white, purple, pink, baby's breath,
stem and leaf

grown for fathers
to pluck, hold, walk the blocks home
and set in a jelly jar on the table,
our small lamps in our small rooms.

I am surprised
to find myself among them, men
who move like my father, I am
overjoyed to be part of this roughened face
studying each arrangement for the one
I will carry home.

What The Parent Daydreams About

If, say, this very moment,
we were winked away to Paris,
I dare say
            my right hand
would be just to the north
of your easternmost kneecap.

Yes, Eiffel; yes, Seine, Champs-Elysées, pan au chocolat;
but

my right hand would
be about halfway
up your coast,

your dress
dancing tangos
with my socks, we,
not worried

if our room views
Sacra Coeur or Notre Dame because

my left hand, your west hand,
your south and east and north,

your lips
hot and bright
as all the skies
fall
in storms
on mine.

Bird Watching

That bird, Sophia, on the fencepost there,
black as night but for each shoulder's bright stripe,
is a red winged blackbird.

It's no eagle or ostrich, you can see it's only big
as my fist; but one time one snuck up
while your dad was on his ten-speed along the orchards
        and cornfields

on an empty morning road under a sky like an upside
        down ocean
and tapped him on his head.

You do not know this yet,
but the sky does not do this.

So as your father's windy daydreams broke
and he swerved his head to see
which apocalypse or mythology or Finger of God was
        motioning for his attention

he did not see the pickup chugging down the other way,
brown boxes of green apples stacked;

he only saw black,
wings rushing in a black halo, red smudge
chasing that sheen through the air.

Bird watchers watch
for ivory-billed woodpeckers,
for kakapos, kokakos, and black-breasted pufflegs,

they don't set up their folding chairs in fields
to observe these birds
who sit on every fence-wire on every country road.

But your father will tell you, Sophia,
it is the most remarkable bird you may ever see,
its colors blurred against the blue
as the end of the world billows just inches from your ear.

RESPONSE TO DENISE DUHAMEL'S POEM
"Napping on the Afternoon of My Thirty-ninth Birthday"

My daughter is almost two.
Her favorite book, *Corduroy's Birthday*,
is about a toy bear
and his birthday party.

She sings, "Happy
to you, happy
to you" at the page where stuffed animal friends in party hats
sing to Corduroy.

When you tell the rapist in your dream,
"You are my nightmare,"
he buys you ice cream.
That is his device.

Men, people,
mostly men,
are like that. I tell this
to my daughter.

She keeps singing,
"Happy
to you."
God bless her.

She grows
into her woman
body, meets men
from nightmares and daydreams.

At the movies, smooth trolls
sit between her and the husband
she would hopefully meet,
not yet knowing

how to decipher
one from the other,
hopefully starting to suspect
she has the grace to prance with you and your gossamer
        friends.

Her dreams
are tough to interpret, too.
The other night, she woke
shaking, stuttering, stumbling to say something;

finally, she sobbed: "Gwasses!"
trying to sound out her fears
with the handful of nouns
she can hold in her stubby fingers.

It's like, imagine you're in a foreign land
and Jesus tells you to build an ark:
you run into the street
knowing how to ask for a toilet and for one of the
        chocolate breads please.

It took an hour to calm her
back to sleep. I will send you a photo of her.
She has a big round butt, a pudgy little waist,
and she is so very, very lovely.

Please tell her this
should you pass her in that long, red lobby
of the multiplex where dreamers go
for their late night shows.

We Rarely Pause, Now, to Contemplate How in Love We Are

Remember
how we once occupied so many hours, we
counting how we made out with X
for so many minutes,

how substantially we
missed them when they dumped us
or went on vacation or left
the room, do you remember

counting every strand of color in their pupils,
the flush of your heart, the hurricane
in your stomach when you first asked them out,
asked for forgiveness, asked to be taken back, asked them to
        marry you?

What a wonder, now, after so much drama, this
happily ever after,
writing poems
through the spirals your daughter drew on every page in your
        notebook,

lines curving
like twelfth century decorative flourish,
lending your words some sort of
official or religious clarity.

And, at the end of the day,
Little Mermaid finally turned off
and daughter away in her bed,
hold your now-wife's hand, sit

quietly on the sofa;
stare out the windows into
worlds waiting for light
to draw back their shapes,

and hold
with a quietness you didn't know
your heart, accustomed to shouting, had
in those days when time itself

began, heaven both impossibly distant
and pressed up against you and,
now,
fading like fog into a landscape

which glows into the heavens
so softly
you almost fail
to notice.

NOTE TO A FRIEND: THE LONG, DARK NIGHT OF YOUR DATING LIFE

So for months or years at a time; you dated one,
then the next, then the next, then the next;

but they were difficult–which is code for insane–
and, over time, everyone moved on to become friends

or acquaintances, or at least now when you might run
into one another, nobody yells, "I hate you!"

and you find yourself
toying with those memories

the way you once toyed with volatile chemicals in
        Chemistry classes
with:

"am I fat?" "am I uglier than their new love?"
"are these really my thighs?" "I'm not the crazy one, am
        I?"

Yes.
Yes, yes, and yes. And also no.

Put the cork back in, Romeo; no shish kabob tonight,
        Juliet;
you're just, what, late twenties, thirties,

and the tide on your dating shores went out early,
earlier than you expected, leaving you

with a beach full of jellyfish and driftwood and you
screaming, "How am I gonna build a life out of all this
        trash!?"

as if the universe itself is finding inventive ways
just to make you miserable;

and you are the struggling salmon, you
are Leonardo DiCaprio shivering in the water while
        Celine Dion sings, you

are bound by the gods' command
to suffer.

Well,
you can let it go, little Sisyphus;

you've just been listening to friends who only told you the
        encouraging part,
tossing you vague bon bons like: "Be yourself,

and everything will fall into place,"
and, well, unicorn, didn't you then sit at the bar thinking,
        "I

am being myself," meticulously dressed
as yourself, hyper-aware that you are you, comfortable all
        by yourself

being yourself; hoping that that special other will notice
how much you desperately

don't
need them and come over and say: "Hi."

Though you try not to think this as you're
supposed to be so goddamn happy being yourself that
        yourself don't need them and their

soft,
shimmering...

Maybe yourself
was the problem, maybe you just need to forget it, buy that
        motorcycle,

invest everything you've got into becoming world champion
at Scrabble,

get every one of your friends in on a three-month
        nonrefundable bike tour of Belgium,
because only then,

when it will
completely

screw your life up,
can the cosmos work

their peculiar machinations,
can the stars line up like the fruits of your desires

across the slot machine screen
above

on this dark, dark,
beautiful night,

so dark
you can finally see

every light there is
in this long valley

that is
your

home.

DRIVING ACROSS SOUTH DAKOTA

The car skims past lakes
of corn sheaves, sunshine
dripping off stalk-stubs.

Silos are ships in the distance,
stacks rising to stroke horizons.
Driving across South Dakota

makes me regret
the meditation time I spend
on TV and email instead, the corn

and tomatoes I didn't have at lunch.
South Dakota, the signs
floating in your fields ask me

to live better,
to thank God, to spend
time with my wife and daughter;

I am surprised
how presumptuous you've grown, Dakota,
but, I admit,

you know me
surprisingly well;
I assure you

I
am hurrying
home.

Bed Poem

I love this, now,
no baby between us
thrashing in her dreams,
tiny Atlas with feet on Earth, palms on sky–
though I doubt Atlas kicked so much.

I love, when I lie down,
we are both drifting in the same ocean,
our sides together or your thigh
over my belly or our feet touching at the horizon
where all roads appear to meet

because even if we, by morning,
are two buoys bobbing on waves, we
are tied, our bells ring
in a sound familiar now
as our own breathing

Little Lamb, Who Made Thee? Dost Thou Know Who Made Thee? I Did Dammit!

Two year olds don't respond
to logical requisitions, don't follow
chains of command, don't understand
the efficacy of paperwork and protocol.

When they decide
they do not wish to change
a swollen diaper, no matter
how far across the room you can smell it,

you can explain the benefits
of clean underthings all you want, you can
show every graph and flowchart in the western world
on proper prevention of diaper rash.

She will not care.
You can plead and entreat,
stand over her with the implicit menace
of adult mass,

but she will not cower.
She dares to defy your imperialist threats of bourgeois
        parentism,
she cries for liberte, egalite, and fraternite,
she announces an end to your oppressive, ageist regime!

And you might admire her
in your other life, but here,
in this situation, you
are the George Wallace, Richard Nixon, King George, Louis
        XVI, guy driving the tank in Tiananmen Square,

your face red, your power
fleeting, you suddenly visualize all your statues toppled,
all your palaces in ashes, the fate of the world
in one poopy Pamper, she

shrieking, "Gaaaaaa no no no, no no no!"
in the way which can only mean "USA out of our diapers!"
her fist in the air, she will not fold,
she will overcome

some
day.

Advanced Lessons in the Old Testament

So I bought my daughter a toy vacuum
unlike any other; it
blinked and flashed, had twelve different sounds and
        practically danced, and she
built forts with and painted on the box it came in,
ignored the toy itself
until it proved the perfect machine to run over the dog's
        toes with
over and over and over, beeping and booping and
        chugging
as the dog quaked in terror;

when such a marvel
sits on top of the fridge, in full sight
but untouchable, only then
can she desire it, oh,

as a son, myself, I never quite got
that Father
selling his own children into servitude, starvation,
molestation, genocide, taking away Paradise
over an apple, I
always wanted that New Testament daddy,
the one with the mercy and the love and the kumbaya, my
        Lord, kumbay-freaking-ya;

but I now appreciate
the need to shout things like:
"I cast thee out!"

because I now get
telling your chosen people again and again what to do

only to see them screw around and not do it, I have said
        it:
"Do not stand like that on the couch's arm, you'll fall and
        hurt yourself," "Do
not stand like that on the couch's arm, you'll fall and hurt
        yourself," "Do not
stand like that on the couch's arm, you'll fall and hurt
        yourself!"

only to hear the "thud," the cry, the howl, I
will see you turned to salt so fast it'll drown your world,
        kid.

That's not saying I don't know
the seeing her in her pain
and feeling your heart curl
in a sort of shame. You, then, will do
anything: tear open the seas, light the sky like a torch,
        make frogs fall like rain,
if it will see her free;

and when you raise your face out
from the oceans you've wept into your palms

and see your daughter
poking at the dog with a butterfly net, then one quick flourish
        of a fake poke after you snarl at her to stop, oh,
crack those tablets to dust, shrivel that manna back to rock,
        wish her luck spinning figure-eights through the
        desert,

for I, as a son, have always reached for a God of healing
        and forgiveness,
of light and peace and lasting hope, but I

am now the father,
understand
the love
of the holy,
burning
wrath.

February: Letter From a Friend
After Fifteen Years

The email from Christine was about our friend Linda,
in the hospital and not
doing well. I'll save you
the details. What I offer to tell
is that my three-year old daughter can't sleep tonight
because she finally noticed at church
how a man's body hangs grotesquely
off the planks of the cross. She can't sleep,
wanting to ask about Jesus
and death, how he died, what bad man did this,
was he thirsty or hungry, where are his friends, his
            mommy, his daddy, am I
going to die and leave her
alone.   As
you can imagine,
my answers
are less than awesome, stumbling more
the steadier they struggle to sound; I try
describing Easter
in a way that makes sense
to her, in a way that makes sense
to me. And she finds calm
in the word "Easter,"
thinking about chocolate
and, for some reason, our dog Panda. I think
of you tonight, Linda, I pray
for Easter to interrupt this long cold, I pray
to come see California again soon
and visit, my daughter chasing your sons

in a kitchen, yellow roses in a vase on the counter,
their smell crackling in the air
all that we can conjure
from the word "Easter"
bringing us back.

Notes For My Daughter Against Chasing Storms

Tornadoes swing through like a kid
playing hopscotch, rip one house to splinters
and leave the neighbors unmussed,
up and down, here and there,
they flatten churches on Easter Sunday,
take up whole towns by the roots,
drive a piece of straw into a tree,
stick a single two by four into a roof
and declare it "art," stack a car
on a car on a motorcycle,
call it a night.

And that, my daughter, is how teenage boys approach love.
I don't say that it is
evil, more like an amoral force of nature,
they look all pleasant showers before they
tear your roof off and leave
your trees in shreds.
So you may dream of his blue
eyes, cloud-free compliments, the music
he likes, the motorcycle he drives,
the great tattoos on his neck, but

when the skies turn that yellow, that green,
when the hail starts popping through air
fit to boil, you listen
to my forecast, you leave the car
parked, grab a flashlight
with one hand, a blanket with the other, go
for the basement, now you run.

CHAPTER 3

THE HAPPILY EVER AFTER

isn't what you imagined,
book on the nightstand, sheets pulled up to your chin.
          The tales
of how they meet are so
vivid, visceral, so full of abandon
with every dragon slain, every trap
impossibly sidestepped,
the gnomish man with his clickety spindle
left tricked and shamed, each deer heart
returned wet in a box, witches
shot out of the forests like cannonballs,
all the mountains, all the oceans, all of the skies
woven into the story that
is how
it starts.

Now

even their names
have been taken away
not by dwarves or ninjas or strange voices howling from
          their oatmeal bowls
but necessity, practicality, "Mommy,"
"Daddy," Prince Charming sometimes breaks, he once
          held up the baby
who wouldn't stop crying, tightened his fingers around it
          and growled
"I
hate
you,"
it is not
out of cruelty, no,
just for the same reasons she, when no one is around,

will set her tiara with a click on the steps
and weep into her knees;

the galleons
are not burned, not swept off course by thundering waves
to wash ashore on islands of riddles to unravel,
they do not spend years pining and wondering where, oh
          where their other is and would they see them again.
The galleon is a Hyundai
and it's right there,
bobbing in the harbor. There are

dishes, there is laundry, the carpet is wet
again, the frying pan has been in the sink for three days,
parent teacher conferences and
commute to work, this
is part of ever, part of after, this,
like that misshapen gear is somehow part of the watch, is
          part
of happily, this

is where the story gets absolutely
daring though the printers ran out of ink
dozens of chapters back;
the flying horses, the talking swords, the singing pirates,
          chupacabras, the goddamn gumdrop cabanas
          filled with some horrible secrets, smells, and
          haberdashery
are all passed,

this

is where you realize
slipping past the troll, turning the ghost to stone
was nothing

compared not
to how you came together
but to how
you managed
to stay.

About the Author

MATT MASON has won a Pushcart Prize and two Nebraska Book Awards (for Poetry in 2007 and Anthology in 2006); organized and run poetry programming with the U.S. Department of State in Kathmandu, Nepal and Minsk, Belarus; and been on five teams at the National Poetry Slam. He is executive director of the Nebraska Writers Collective, has served as board president of the Nebraska Center for the Book, and is the Nebraska State Coordinator for Poetry Out Loud, a Poetry Foundation/ NEA program. He edits **PoetryMenu.com**, a listing of every Nebraska poetry event. Matt lives in Omaha with his wife, the poet Sarah McKinstry-Brown, and daughters Sophia and Lucia.

CPSIA information can be obtained
at www.ICGtesting.com
Printed in the USA
LVHW112355040719
623233LV00001B/11/P